THE HOLY SPIRIT
AT WORK TODAY

By

John F. Walvoord

$1.25

Special printing through arrangement with Moody Press by

Back to the Bible Broadcast

Box 82808   Lincoln, Nebraska 68501

ACKNOWLEDGMENT

Chapters 1-5 are reprinted, with changes, from the series of articles, "Contemporary Issues in the Doctrine of the Holy Spirit," *Bibliotheca Sacra* 130-31 (1973-74), by permission of the publisher.

ISBN: 0-8024-5297-3

(5-3420—85M—54)

Printed in the United States of America

Contents

Introduction

THIS STUDY of the work of the Spirit in the church and the world today originated in a series of lectures delivered at several schools and churches and in a series of articles in *Bibliotheca Sacra* in which an attempt was made to summarize the work of the Holy Spirit in the peculiar context of our modern world. The goal of the presentation was to state biblical teaching rather than to survey modern literature, and to correct misunderstandings and misguided emphases in the doctrine of the Holy Spirit.

For the most part the twentieth century has focused on human experience rather than theology. The rise of existentialism, with its emphasis on present experience and present values, has tended to downgrade history and biblical revelation of the past as well as to ignore prophecy and the future. The tendency has been to exalt present experience as the main source of truth. This has given rise to neoorthodoxy with its dependence on present revelation, to the charismatic movement with its emphasis on speaking in tongues and divine healing, and more recently to the growing interest in mystical experience and experimentation in the occult, which is part of the increasing influence of demonism in contemporary experience. All of these trends and movements have tended to ignore and obscure the timeless truths that relate to the doctrine of the Spirit as revealed in the Scripture.

Contemporary literature has tended to confuse rather than clarify the issues. Most of the books dealing with the Holy Spirit have assumed that the Scriptures are not the final authority and that our only hope of determining truth in relation to the Holy Spirit is contemporary experience. Accordingly, while there have been many new books, there has been little new light. A study of contemporary literature on the Holy Spirit is singularly unproductive in helping one to arrive at the real truth concerning the work of the Holy Spirit.

This present study is a restatement of biblical truth concerning the work of the Holy Spirit. In one sense it is not new, but the doctrine of the Spirit is presented in its modern context. It is intended to serve laymen, pastors, and missionaries seeking clarification in their understanding of the work of the Holy Spirit today. This study does not include consideration of the person of the Holy Spirit or many of the formal theological problems related to technical theology; and it is not intended to replace the author's earlier work on *The Holy Spirit* (Grand Rapids: Zondervan, 1958), which is a theological textbook dealing with the person and work of the Holy Spirit.

Because there is such widespread confusion on the work of the Holy Spirit, this presentation of the five major areas of the work of the Spirit today is intended to define the major issues in the truth relating to the Holy Spirit.

1

The Spirit at Work in Revealing Truth

THE TWENTIETH CENTURY has been a period of rapid change. The advent of the atomic bomb, rapid communication and travel, and multiplied social and economic problems have set the present age apart from any similar period of history. The modern mind accordingly is asking new questions about what God is saying to our generation. In theology especially, the leading questions are, How does God speak to man and What is He saying today?

In discussing the nature of divine revelation to man, one is approaching the central questions of theology and philosophy. The problem is first of all related to the nature of God. If God is infinite in His wisdom and is the Creator of all things, He is obviously greater than what He created. The question must be faced as to whether such a Creator would desire to communicate to His creatures. Those who believe in God as Creator generally believe that He created for the purpose of revealing Himself and to display His infinite perfections. This explains how God has revealed Himself in nature.

In the creation of man, God deliberately made a being with intellect (mind), sensibility (feeling), and will (power of moral choice). Man, although on a finite plane, was made like God, and therefore was the kind of creature to whom God could communicate. Under these circumstances—God being what He is and man being created in the image and likeness of God—communication between them would seem possible and reasonable.

Into this picture, however, came the problem of sin with its dulling of man's sensitivity to divine revelation and a natural blindness to truth about God. It is because man is a sinful creature that a need arises for a special work of God to make divine communication to man effective. This introduces and makes necessary the role of the Holy Spirit as the divine Communicator of truth to man.

REVELATION IN NATURE

The universe as a product of divine creation is one of the important means of divine revelation to man. According to Romans 1:20, "The invisible things of him from the creation of the world are clearly seen, being understood by the things that are made, even his eternal power and Godhead." The universe in its immensity, complexity, design, and beauty testify to the God who created it; and as Romans bring out, it is a testimony to the power of God and to the personality and deity of God. This revelation of God in nature, which is perceivable by man in his normal intelligence, is stated in Romans to be so clear that according to Romans 1:20, "they are without excuse," that is, all men should worship the Creator. This is the ground of condemnation of the heathen world. Scripture frequently calls attention to the wonder of the created universe as a display of the glory of God. Psalm 19 is an excellent illustration of this, beginning with the familiar statement, "The heavens declare the glory of God; and the firmament sheweth his handywork."

The revelation of God in nature is such that even man in his fallen condition is held accountable for this display of the perfections of God. Christians who are aided by the indwelling Holy Spirit can appreciate more than others how beautiful and significant the natural world is. However, even an unsaved person should be able to recognize the testimony of nature to its Creator. It is an illustration of the utter sinfulness of man that, although he finds evidence of human personality behind anything that man makes, too often he is willing to ignore the evidence that God created the world. This blindness of man is held in Scripture to be without excuse and a proper basis for divine judgment of man.

REVELATION IN THE BIBLE

All that is implied in revelation in the natural world is stated explicitly in the Scriptures. Within orthodoxy, the claim of Scripture to be inspired of God is accepted as the explanation of this supernatural revelation.

According to the central passage of 2 Timothy 3:16, "All scripture is given by inspiration of God, and is profitable for doctrine, for reproof, for correction, for instruction in righteousness." This passage teaches that the Scriptures were breathed by God. This means that the authors were the channels of divine revelation and the Scriptures were something that God produced through human instruments. It is because of this that Scriptures are authoritative and the only infallible rule for faith and practice. Inspiration extends to all Scripture, to every word and every phrase, and therefore assures the factual accuracy of what is said.

As indicated in connection with oral revelation in 2 Peter 1:20-21, the revelation of divine truth was possible because "holy men of God spake as they were moved [borne along] by the Holy Ghost." All who are willing to accept the Bible as the Word of God recognize that inspiration is a work of the Holy Spirit and that the Scriptures would have been impossible apart from this supernatural ministry of the Holy Spirit.

The proofs for the inspiration of the Bible are both internal and external. There is abundant testimony of Old Testament writers to their belief that they were writing by inspiration (2 Sa 23:2-3; Is 59:21; Jer 1:9). The terminology of the prophets and the expressions such as, "Thus saith the Lord," as found in hundreds of instances, testify to the hand of God in the production of the Scriptures. The very titles of the Bible.

such as "the Word of the Lord," "thy Word," and similar expressions, are found over a hundred times in the Old Testament, and in many cases refer to direct quotations of what God has actually said and in other cases to what the prophets said as God's representatives (Ps 107:11, 119:11; Pr 30:5). Hundreds of prophecies were made in the Bible; and when these were fulfilled, often with minute accuracy as for instance in the birth of Christ in Bethlehem (Mic 5:2), it serves to prove that the Bible, unlike any other book in the world, is accurate in its prophecies. As about one-fourth of the Bible was prediction of future events when it was written, fulfillment of prophecy becomes an important proof of the inspiration of the Bible.

One of the most decisive evidences for inspiration is the testimony of Christ to the Scriptures. Often, in quoting the Old Testament, Christ affirmed that it was inspired of the Spirit—as in Matthew 22:42-43 and Mark 12:36 quoting Psalm 110:1. In the New Testament as a whole, the apostles frequently quoted from the Old Testament, indicating their belief that it was inspired of God—as in Peter's quotation of Psalm 41:9 in Acts 1:16, and in the quotation of Psalm 2 in Acts 4:24-25. Paul quotes Isaiah 6:9-10 in Acts 28:25. Similar references may be seen in Hebrews 3:7 and 10:15-16. These sample indications of common recognition by Christ and the apostles of the inspiration of the Old Testament, as well as the claim of inspiration of the New Testament in 1 Timothy 5:18—quoting Deuteronomy 25:4 and Luke 10:7—and 2 Peter 3:16 referring to Paul's epistles as Scripture, tend to support the claim of inspiration of both Testaments.

Inspiration extends to all forms of Scripture and relates to the unknown past, to history, to moral and religious law, to devotional literature, to the contemporary prophetic message, as well as to the eschatological portions dealing with prophecy of the future. Inspiration extends equally to all kinds of Scripture, whether direct quotation from God or whether the statements of men, and is the basis for the conclusion that the Bible is factually true. The abundant evidence in support of the inspiration of the Bible, which is discussed here only briefly, is so extensive that some of the finest scholars of all time have found this evidence quite sufficient to affirm the infallibility and inspiration of the entire sixty-six books of the Bible.

Historically and logically, belief in the Bible has been inseparable from faith in the person and work of Jesus Christ, and unbelief in relation to the inspired Word of God has inevitably also questioned the validity of Christ, the incarnate Word of God. The proofs for the one are proofs for the other.

REVELATION TO MAN IN BIBLE TIMES

In addition to revealing Himself through the written Word, it is clear from Scripture that God gave man special divine revelation. God often spoke to individuals, revealing Himself, His will for them, and His direction for their lives, apart from Scripture itself. Two large books of the Bible, Genesis and Job, record numerous instances of such direct communication with man from Adam to Moses and contain allusions to general knowledge of God which must have come by special divine revelation. Important truths such as the nature of God, His moral law, His purpose for man in time, and His plan for man in eternity were revealed to man in this way.

The extent of such divine revelation is illustrated in the book of Genesis where God spoke to Adam, Enoch, and Noah. Abraham is an outstanding illustration of the period before Scripture was written of one to whom God gave broad revelation concerning his posterity, his title to the Holy Land, and the broad purpose of God to produce through Abraham blessing to the entire world, fulfilled in Christ and in the Scriptures. Moses was given detailed revelation, recorded in the Pentateuch, for the guidance and direction of the nation Israel. Throughout Old Testament times, God raised up many prophets who delivered divine messages to their generation, only portions of which have been preserved in the Bible. The outstanding personalities of Samuel, David, Isaiah, Jeremiah, Ezekiel, Daniel, the minor prophets, and many of the psalmists (some of them unnamed), were used of God to declare His message. The basic method of special revelation alongside written Scripture is continued in the New Testament, much on the same pattern as found in the Old Testament but with more explicit testimony to the ministry of the Holy Spirit.

Divine revelation was given in various ways. Sometimes God appears to have spoken to man as if He were a man Himself and communication was in words. This was true in the case of God's relationship with Adam as well as with many who followed. A second means of revelation was through dreams, of which there are many instances in the Bible (Gen 20:3-7; 31:10-13, 24; 37:5-20; 40:5-16; 41:11-13, 15-32; 42:9). Even after Scripture began to be written, dreams continued to be used in some cases as a means of divine revelation (Num 12:6; Dan 2:1-35; 4:1-18; 7:1-14). Along with dreams were visions as a means of revealing divine truth—in which case the word "seer," or one who sees visions, became characteristic of prophetic revelation. Illustrations are Isaiah's experience (Is 1:1; 6:1), Ezekiel's experience (Eze 1:3), Daniel's visions (Dan 8:1-27; 9:20-27; 10:1—12:13), and Micaiah's vision of heaven (1 Ki 22:19). A similar method was that of trances, as in Ezekiel 8:3 and 11:24. Whatever the means of divine revelation, the important point is that God sought by supernatural means to communicate Himself.

Divine revelation, of course, received a tremendous addition when Jesus Christ came in the flesh. He was a revelation of God in His person and life as well as in His prophetic utterances. Throughout the apostolic period, special revelation continued as God communicated truth to individuals and to churches. The Lord appeared, for instance, in a vision to Stephen in Acts 7:55-56, to Paul in Acts 9:3-9 (see also Ac 26:13-19), and to Ananias relative to his relationship to Paul (Ac 9:10-16). Cornelius was given a vision in Acts 10 in relation to Peter. Peter also was given a vision of his relationship with Cornelius in the same chapter. Another illustration is found in Acts 11:28 in the revelation given to Agabus of the coming famine. Many other illustrations could be cited, including the special revelation given to Paul in Acts 27:21-26 and in the vision of 2 Corinthians 12:1-7. The whole book of Revelation records the special revelation given to John.

From these many instances it is clear that God is not limited as to the means and channels of divine revelation, and in each case the means of revelation is suited to the end.

REVELATION TO MAN TODAY

The major problem in the contemporary doctrine of revelation relates to the nature and extent of divine revelation today apart from the facts of revelation found in the Bible. In a word, does God give special revelation today as He did in the Old and New Testament periods? To what extent does God communicate directly to those who are believers in the Lord Jesus Christ?

One aspect of contemporary revelation is the teaching ministry of the Holy Spirit, predicted by Christ (Jn 16:12-15). As discussed in 1 Corinthians 2:9—3:2, the Holy Spirit teaches by illuminating the Scriptures, making the revelation of God understandable. While the natural man cannot understand spiritual truth, the spiritual man is taught the meaning of Scripture by the Holy Spirit. Such revelation, however, does not go beyond what is actually in the text of Scripture.

It is understood in contemporary theology that God can give guidance today. Guidance does not necessarily require an additional revelation but is rather the application of the Scriptures in general principles to the particular need of the individual seeking direction from God. Guidance is not in itself infallible, although God never misguides a person. Christians, however, can misinterpret guidance and can misunderstand God's directions. Further, guidance is never normative;

that is, what God guides one to do may not be what He will guide another to do. It is part of the personal ministry of the Holy Spirit to show the individual what the will of God is for him (Ro 12:1-2); and being led by the Spirit is one of the marks of being a Christian (Ro 8:14). The guidance of the Spirit is personal and adapted to God's individual purpose for the individual life and, as such, is in contrast to general law (Gal 5:18).

The particular problem that arises in contemporary study of revelation by the Holy Spirit is whether the Holy Spirit can give normative truth suitable for formulation of doctrine apart from explicit teaching of this truth in the Bible. Here in a word is the issue between orthodoxy and neoorthodoxy, between the historic doctrine of revelation in the church and the contemporary teaching of Barth, Brunner, and Reinhold Niebuhr and many others. In order to understand the issues, a brief review must be undertaken of the background of this movement, its premises, and its conclusions.

Liberal theology in the early twentieth century had reduced the Bible to a natural record of religious experience and to various degrees had eliminated its supernatural element as well as its authority. The transcendent God who had created the universe was replaced by an immanent God indistinguishable from the process of evolution and for all practical purposes pantheistic in His relation to creation. Such a view left little room for a divine doctrine of supernatural revelation, a real communication between an infinite God and finite man, or other concepts taught in the Bible. Revelation was simply human discovery on a natural plane.

Liberal theology was challenged by Karl Barth in his *Epistle to the Romans* published in 1918. Karl Barth found that the naturalistic doctrines of liberalism did not meet the needs of men in war time, and he concluded that the problem was that a supernatural form of communication was required between God and man. Although this was naturally impossible, Barth asserted that God did speak directly to man although this constituted nobody as an infallible prophet.

Barth also reasserted that God was transcendent and man was sinful and finite. In revealing Himself to man, the incarnate Christ is the supreme fact of divine revelation; but according to Barth, revelation is not something to be put on paper but something experienced personally by the individual.

Although Barth did not accept the infallibility of Scripture, the historicity of Adam, or any detailed prophetic revelation, he nevertheless opposed liberalism in many points. Barth seems to have accepted the virgin birth of Christ, the deity of Christ, the death of Christ on the cross, and His bodily resurrection. Most of his followers, however, did not go as far as Barth in reasserting these doctrines.

The difficulties confronting Barth's neoorthodox interpretation of revelation are evident in contemporary theology. Neoorthodoxy lacks any norm for divine truth as it is based on individual experience. Hence, there is a wide variety of doctrines held by those who are neoorthodox. Even their doctrine of Christ tends to be their experience of Christ rather than the Christ of Scripture and history. The whole concept that God can speak clearly and authoritatively in communicating divine truth to man today apart from the Scripture is highly questionable. Neoorthodoxy to date has not been able to produce one normative truth not already taught in the Bible. Accordingly, it must be concluded that neoorthodoxy actually is a serious and deceptive error, even though it includes some doctrines which are orthodox.

God is speaking today—speaking through nature and speaking through the Bible—and guiding man in his daily life. Primarily, however, God speaks to man through the Scriptures, and He does not reveal normative truth except as it is already revealed in the Scriptures themselves. The test of truth must remain not what man experiences today but what the Scriptures have stated long ago.

2

The Spirit at Work in Spiritual Renewal

A TREMENDOUS UPHEAVAL has occurred in the twentieth century in regard to morality. In previous generations it was taken almost for granted that man could solve his problems. The advance of science and health, the development of educational programs, the spread of democracy, and the proclamation of the Christian gospel were considered sufficient to bring in ultimately a utopia for man. It was thought that it would take only time and application of these principles to solve the basic problems of man.

In the period following World War II, however, it has become increasingly evident that moral deterioration instead of improvement seems to mark our generation. The rapid advance of crime, youth delinquency, increase in divorce, exploitation of sex, and extensive use of dope has spread like a cancer through modern society. Today there is widespread skepticism as to whether the situation can be improved. Youth is in revolt against the civilization which was inherited from its parents, and parents despair in attempting to solve the problems of their children. Increased international tensions caused by the struggle between Communism and the noncommunistic world, race tensions all over the world, and increasing rebellion against poverty and malnutrition seem to mark our present generation. It is becoming evident that man is not able to solve his own problems, and that only a divine or theological solution provides the answers. Society is desperately sick because the individuals who compose it are becoming more and more depraved.

Few facts of contemporary experience are more evident than the fact of man's sinfulness and depravity. Even in non-Christian points of view, the prevailing opinion now recognizes that man is far from what he ought to be and needs renewal if he is going to find the utmost in human experience and realization of his role in life. In Christian thought, especially in orthodox circles, the sinfulness of man is taken as evident in life as well as in Scriptures. One of the main purposes of Christianity is to bring renewal to man who is enslaved by sin and separated from God by both his nature and his acts.

Christianity in large measure can be defined as the application of a divine remedy for man in his depravity. The process of salvation originates in God, is proclaimed by man, and is mediated by the Holy Spirit. Although there is little question within orthodox Christianity of the basic tenets of man's fall into sin and God's provision of salvation, the precise details of God's program still are often blurred in modern religious literature, and it is necessary to gain perspective in the understanding of God's program of salvation and renewal for man.

The broad program of God for renewal of man in salvation may be divided into three areas: (1) new life in the Spirit; (2) a new divine program—the new society in Christ; and (3) a new divine power—the presence of the Spirit, which provides enablement for life and service.

NEW LIFE IN THE SPIRIT

The Scriptures clearly testify to the fact that man is spiritually dead and lacks any spiritual life apart from salvation in Christ. The state of spiritual death is spelled out in detail in Romans 5:12-21, and the dictum is given: "Death passed upon all men, for that all have sinned" (Ro 5:12). According to 1 Corinthians 15:22, "in Adam all die." The Ephesian Christians are declared to have been "dead in trespasses and sins" prior to their experience of salvation (Eph 2:1). It is because of this universal lack of eternal life that Nicodemus, the religious Jew, was informed by Christ, "Ye must be born again" (Jn 3:7).

The state of spiritual death did not completely erase the divine image, however, and man can manifest religious yearning for God, prompted by the Spirit of God, even before he is converted. It is nevertheless true that apart from the work of the Holy Spirit in bestowing grace, there seems to be no natural stirring in the human heart toward God. Man is spiritually dead and does not originate in himself a movement toward God and spiritual life.

Spiritual renewal begins when man is prompted by the Spirit of God, brought under conviction of need, and made aware of the provision of salvation in Christ (Jn 16:7-11). While the work of grace in the heart of one spiritually dead is inscrutable, it is nevertheless effective in somehow supernaturally bringing one who is spiritually dead to the point of active faith in Jesus Christ, resulting in his salvation.

The new life in Christ which is the basis for spiritual renewal is described in Scripture under three figures. In the gospel of John, it is approached from the standpoint of bestowal of eternal life. Early in the gospel the revelation is given that as many as receive Christ by faith become the children of God with the result that they are born spiritually, not of natural blood nor of natural will but born of God (Jn 1:12-13).

This is brought out further in the conversation of Christ with Nicodemus in John 3 where Nicodemus, the religious ruler of the Jews, is flatly told, "Except a man be born again, he cannot see the kingdom of God" (Jn 3:3). Christ further explained, "Except a man be born of water and of the Spirit, he cannot enter into the kingdom of God" (Jn 3:5). He defines this new birth as being "born of the Spirit" (Jn 3:6). As the chapter proceeds, emphasis is given to faith in Jesus Christ as the means of eternal life. As embodied in the familiar text of

John 3:15-16, there can be no valid spiritual renewal until there is bestowal of eternal life on one who formerly was spiritually dead. This begins the moment an individual trusts in Jesus Christ as his Saviour.

The resulting new life is described under a second figure in John 5:25 where Christ said, "Verily, verily, I say unto you, The hour is coming, and now is, when the dead shall hear the voice of the Son of God: and they that hear shall live." The new life in Christ received at conversion is compared here to resurrection from the dead. The one who was spiritually dead now becomes spiritually alive. The same figure is expounded in Romans 6:13 where Christians are described as "those that are alive from the dead" and who, therefore, are called to live as those spiritually resurrected. The Ephesian Christians are also reminded of their spiritual resurrection in the statement that although they "were dead in sins," yet they are now "quickened" [made alive] and "raised up" to be with Christ in the heavenlies (Eph 2:5-6). The nature of resurrection is supernatural, and it is a work of divine power. Spiritual renewal accordingly is a divine miracle in which that which was dead is now alive.

A third figure used to describe spiritual renewal is embraced in the idea of creation. According to Ephesians 2:10, "We are his workmanship, created in Christ Jesus unto good works, which God hath before ordained that we should walk in them." The central passage on this approach is found in 2 Corinthians 5:17 where the statement is made, "Therefore, if any man be in Christ, he is a new creature: old things are passed away; behold, all things are become new." The contrast is between the old creation—what man is in his fallen state in Adam—and what he now is with eternal life in Christ. Just as the inanimate dust of the earth was formed by God and became alive when God breathed into it the breath of life, so man dead in trespasses and sins becomes alive by an act of divine creation which

establishes the renewed man in a new order of being. As a part
of the work of God in creating man anew, man is now appointed unto good works which man in his fallen estate would
not be able to accomplish.

The work of God by the Spirit in spiritual renewal fulfills all
three of these descriptive concepts: man is indeed born as from
above, receiving life from God as his Father; man is spiritually
resurrected and no longer dead in sin; man is a new creation
instead of a member of a fallen creation.

The dramatic moral depravity of contemporary civilization
illustrates graphically the need for just such a spiritual renewal
as is provided by the Spirit in regeneration. Man, sinful by
nature, needs to have the reviving and transforming new life in
Christ. The moral crises of our day confirm what the Scripture has long taught—that man cannot be good apart from a
supernatural work of God in his heart.

The results of the new life in Christ stem from the basic concept of spiritual renewal by bestowal of life. As is true of man
who is born naturally and receives a human nature from his
parents, so man born anew receives a new nature, a new
capacity for service and devotion to God. The new life in
Christ provides new experiences such as spiritual sight instead
of spiritual blindness, spiritual gifts which are added to the
natural gifts, and the capacity for spiritual enjoyment of fellowship with God. Because the new life which is bestowed is eternal, it also provides a new security, for the new life is by nature
eternal. Paul writes the Philippians of "being confident of this
very thing, that he which hath begun a good work in you will
perform it until the day of Jesus Christ" (Phil 1:6). Man is not
simply restored to what he was before the human race fell into
sin, but is now exalted to a new plane of eternal life and security in Christ Jesus. All the spiritual renewal which is possible
for man is founded upon these concepts of a new life, a new
creation, and a new security in Christ.

A NEW DIVINE PROGRAM: THE NEW SOCIETY IN CHRIST

Spiritual renewal for man is not limited to inner transformation and bestowal of life as an individual possession. The work of salvation in man also gives man a new relationship to God and to all those who in like manner have received eternal life from God. This new relationship in the present dispensation which forms a new society in Christ is embodied in the concept of the baptism of the Spirit.

In dispensations prior to the present age of grace, it is clear that man could be born again and could enter into new relationships with fellow believers. It may be assumed that some Gentiles in the Old Testament were rightly related to God by faith, and that many godly Jews realized the peculiar blessings of being related to the nation of Israel racially and yet also related to God's purposes spiritually through new life from God.

In the present age, however, a peculiar work is revealed which did not exist in the Old Testament and apparently will not be realized after the present age. This is the work of God by the Holy Spirit which places a believer *in Christ* and relates him to all fellow believers in the figure of a human body.

In all of the four gospels, John the Baptist is quoted as predicting the future baptism of the Holy Spirit (Mt 3:11; Mk 1:8; Lk 3:16; Jn 1:33). This prophecy was never realized prior to the death, resurrection, and ascension of Christ, but in keeping with the prediction of Christ in Acts 1, it was fulfilled for the first time on the day of Pentecost. Christ had told His disciples prior to His ascension, "John truly baptized with water; but ye shall be baptized with the Holy Ghost not many days hence" (Ac 1:5). Ten days later the promise of the power of the Spirit was fulfilled and with it the baptism of the Spirit.

A careful study of the events of Pentecost will reveal that a number of important ministries of the Spirit were fulfilled in the experience of the apostles on that important day. No doubt they were indwelt by the Spirit as well as filled by the Spirit, but neither of these ministries of the Spirit should be confused with the baptism of the Spirit.

Although the account in Acts 2 does not expressly state that the baptism of the Spirit was inaugurated on that date, it becomes clear from Acts 1:5 and from later passages such as Acts 11:15-17 that the baptism of the Spirit occurred for the first time on the day of Pentecost and subsequently was realized when individuals received Christ as Saviour. Although there has been considerable confusion in evangelical literature between the baptism of the Spirit and other works of the Spirit which occur at the moment of salvation, according to 1 Corinthians 12:13, the baptism of the Spirit should be properly defined as establishing a new position and relationship for all new believers. According to 1 Corinthians 12:13, all believers are baptized into one body by the Spirit of God; hence, the baptism of the Spirit is that which establishes both the place and the relationship of the believer in Christ and in the body of Christ which is composed of all true believers. Baptism is, therefore, positional in that all believers have this position of being in Christ and in the body of Christ, and relational in that, being in this situation, a new relationship is established both to Christ and to all others who are in Christ. It carries with it many important spiritual truths vital to a true comprehension of spiritual renewal in the Holy Spirit.

Among the new relationships and concepts which belong to the doctrine of the baptism of the Holy Spirit is that which was announced by Christ in John 14:20 where Christ said, "At that day ye shall know that I am in my Father, and ye in me, and I in you." The relationship of a believer in Jesus Christ is likened to the relationship of Christ to God the Father and is the ground for the further work of God indwelling the believer embraced in the expression, "I in you."

In the exposition of the doctrine of the baptism of the Spirit in the New Testament, important passages can be cited. The baptism of Romans 6:1-4 is related to the baptism of the Spirit;

and even if the interpretation be followed that this relates to water baptism, it is obvious that the reality that is figured here is that of the baptism of the Spirit. Accordingly, the conclusion may be drawn that because a believer is baptized into Christ and seen by God in this relationship, he is related to what Christ did on the cross, and he is therefore baptized into His death and burial, and he is raised with Christ from the dead. Paul alludes to being "baptized into Christ" in Galatians 3:27, leading to the conclusion that all Christians are "one in Christ Jesus" (Gal 3:28) and through Christ inherit the spiritual promises given to Abraham's spiritual seed—that is, the blessing promised all nations through Abraham (Gal 3:8).

Christians are said to have "one baptism," just as they have "one Lord, one faith" (Eph 4:5). According to Colossians 2:12, the believer is in Christ, is buried with Christ, and is risen with Him. In summary, it may be concluded that the baptism of the Spirit results in a new union with God and with fellow believers, a new position of being in Christ and in the body of Christ, and a new association which is the result of this relationship. The baptism of the Spirit with all of its important results is accordingly an important aspect of the work of the Holy Spirit in spiritual renewal.

A NEW DIVINE POWER: THE PRESENCE OF THE SPIRIT

Simultaneous with the bestowal of new life in the believer and the new relationships established by the baptism of the Spirit is the supreme fact that the believer becomes the temple of God. God the Holy Spirit, as well as God the Father and God the Son, makes the body of the believer His temple on earth.

It is clear that saints prior to the present dispensation had an effective ministry of the Spirit to them. This is described in John 14:17 as the fact that the Spirit "dwelleth with you." A new relationship, however, is announced, and this new relationship of the Spirit is defined by the words, "shall be in you."

Although the Holy Spirit clearly indwelt some saints in the Old Testament, this does not seem to have been universally realized and, in fact, was only bestowed sovereignly by God to accomplish His purpose in certain individuals. The Spirit, being omnipresent, was *with* all those who put their trust in God even if not *in* them, and undoubtedly contributed to their spiritual life and experience. The new relationship is obviously intended to be more intimate and more effective than that which was true before the present dispensation.

Beginning on the day of Pentecost, the promise of Christ that the Holy Spirit "shall be in you" was realized, and the various statements of Christ in John 14 that He would be "in you" (Jn 14:20) were fulfilled. The added revelation, "If a man love me, he will keep my words: and my Father will love him, and we will come unto him, and make our abode with him" (Jn 14:23), indicates that all three Persons of the Trinity indwell the believer in the present age. This indwelling presence of God was anticipated as early as John 7:37-39, where Christ predicted that there would be rivers of living water flowing from within the believer. The explanation attached is that this refers to the Spirit "which they that believe on him should receive."

On the day of Pentecost itself, Peter appealed to those who were present to repent, with the promise, "Ye shall receive the gift of the Holy Ghost" (Ac 2:38). Subsequently this was realized by other believers and is used as a basis for concluding that Cornelius was saved (Ac 11:17), and that the believers in John the Baptist referred to in Acts 19:1-3 were unsaved because they had not yet received the Spirit of God.

The Holy Spirit is mentioned as being given to the believers in Romans 5:5, in 1 Corinthians 2:12, and in 2 Corinthians 5:5, as well as being assumed in many other passages. Unsaved are referred to as those "having not the Spirit" (Jude 19), and even unspiritual Christians such as the Corinthians are assured, "Your body is the temple of the Holy Ghost which is in you, which ye have of God" (1 Co 6:19). Although in the early church there were some delays in the bestowal of the Spirit for appropriate reasons, there can be little doubt that a comprehensive study of the doctrine in the New Testament reveals that every true believer is now indwelt by the Spirit of God.

The presence of the Holy Spirit, as well as the attending presence of God the Father and the Spirit of Christ, is related in Scripture to the important work of spiritual renewal which is subsequent to salvation. According to the Scriptures, the Spirit is the teacher of all truth (Jn 16:13). The Spirit is intended to guide and lead the child of God (Ro 8:14). The presence of the Spirit gives assurance of salvation (Ro 8:16), and His very presence constitutes the evidence that we are sealed unto the day of redemption (Eph 4:30). The sealing of the Spirit is not a work of the Spirit in the ordinary sense and is not something that occurs subsequent to salvation. It is rather that the Holy Spirit Himself is the seal, and His presence is the evidence that is needed to assure the child of God that he really belongs to God and is secure in that relationship until he is completely renewed in body and spirit in the presence of the Lord.

The presence of the Holy Spirit is related to our prayer life, and the Spirit is said to intercede for the believer (Ro 8:26-27). The presence of the Spirit is the secret of the subsequent works of the Spirit, such as the fruit of the Spirit in Galatians 5:22-23, and is the source of power for the use of spiritual gifts. The presence of the Spirit makes possible the command to be filled with the Spirit—which is related to the Spirit in His work in sanctifying—and empowering the believer. The indwelling of the Spirit is in many respects the extension and continuity of the work of God begun in bestowal of life and a new position through baptism of the Spirit. It is the key to the whole subsequent work of sanctification and empowerment of the life of the believer and makes possible a supernatural life that is to the glory of God.

The work of spiritual renewal is accordingly along three major lines. The bestowal of eternal life is the divine remedy for spiritual death. The new position and relationship of the believer as a result of the baptism of the Spirit is the divine step in renewal which remedies the former position of the believer as fallen in Adam. The indwelling divine presence is the provision of God for empowering and enabling the believer to achieve that for which he has been made a new creation. It will have its fulfillment both in time and eternity in which the believer is designed to bring glory to God. The subsequent development of the spiritual life, the achievement of holiness, the use of gifts, and the divine power which is provided for the believer are the extension of the ministries of the Spirit in beginning the spiritual renewal at salvation. The understanding of this and its realization constitute a major aspect of Christian experience and life.

3

The Spirit at Work in the Life of Holiness

THE MORAL CRISIS of contemporary society is a pointed reminder of the need for a new morality. This goal is not achieved by lowering former standards of morality to correspond to present behavior. Such a move is simply to condone immorality and to develop an amoral society. Rather, in harmony with the doctrine of the holiness of God, the goal should be realized of achieving in a new way a morality in keeping with the Scriptures and the character of God. The realization of such a goal is possible only by supernatural power such as is provided by the indwelling presence of the Holy Spirit.

When an individual is spiritually renewed by being born again, he is prepared for a life in the will of God. The believer has (1) a new nature, (2) the life of God in him, (3) a vital relationship to God and to other believers in the baptism of the Spirit, and (4) the presence of God in his body and consciousness. This sets the stage for an effective expression of a life on high moral standards in keeping with the character of God. In this new relationship, a young believer only recently entering into salvation in Christ can nevertheless experience and know the will of God and achieve a high moral standard. Even though immature, a young believer can have a dramatic change in his life. Spiritual maturity, however, is achieved only as the new believer grows in experience. Maturity takes time, whereas spirituality is a possibility for a believer immediately upon conversion.

Although his achievement of moral excellence may always

be relative in this life, it is tied in with the power of the Spirit in his life and the degree to which the Holy Spirit fills him and directs him. A believer now has the power given by God to yield himself to God and be an instrument of righteousness instead of an instrument of sin. The subsequent holy life remains the pattern of experience to be followed today. There are three major factors in this: (1) yieldedness to the Spirit, (2) fellowship with the Spirit, and (3) the ministry of the Spirit.

Yieldedness to the Holy Spirit

The indwelling presence of the Holy Spirit in the believer provides an inexhaustible and constant source of spiritual direction and empowerment. The ministry of the Spirit, however, is not automatic and is not effective without cooperation on the part of the individual, hence the command in 1 Thessalonians 5:19, "Quench not the Spirit." This command, included in a series of other exhortations, puts the finger upon an essential requirement for vital Christian life and conformity to the moral will of God. Quenching is a concept used in relation to extinguishing or suppressing a fire. In Hebrews 11:34 the heroes of faith are said to have "quenched the violence of fire." In the spiritual conflict discussed in Ephesians 6:16, the shield of faith is "able to quench all the fiery darts of the wicked." Hence, it may be concluded that quenching the Holy Spirit is to suppress, stifle, or otherwise obstruct the ministry of the Spirit to the individual. In a word it is saying *no* and replacing the will of the Spirit with the will of the individual. This, in brief, is the whole issue of morality—whether man will accomplish what he wants to do or whether his life is surrendered and yielded to the will of God.

The major conflict of all creation is between the will of God and the will of the creature. This began with the original rebellion of Satan against God outlined in the five "I will's" of Isaiah 14, summarized in the ambitious goal, "I will be like the most high" (Is 14:14). This original act of rebellion against God on the part of Satan was extended to the human race in the Garden of Eden. The conflict of the ages is accordingly between the will of the creature and the will of the Creator.

In order to attain a biblical standard of morality, it is necessary for the believer to be like God, and this involves yieldedness of his own will to the will of God. Accordingly, in Romans 6:13 the exhortation is that we should stop presenting (present tense) our bodies as instruments of unrighteousness, and once for all (aorist tense) present ourselves to God as a single and definite act. In doing this, we should let the Holy Spirit direct our lives and guide our steps and thus achieve the moral standards and goals which are God's will for us.

A similar exhortation is found in Romans 12:1 where the believer is exhorted to present (aorist tense) his body as a living sacrifice once for all and thereby achieve through knowledge and fulfillment "that good, and acceptable, and perfect, will of God" (Ro 12:2). Many believers in Christ have never realistically yielded themselves completely to the will of God, and accordingly their whole life is spent in self-will and self-direction instead of achieving the high standard of fulfillment of the moral and intelligent purpose of God in their lives.

The command of 1 Thessalonians 5:19 is probably best interpreted as, "Stop quenching the Spirit." The implication is that there have been hindrances to the will of the Spirit being established in the life of the believer, and this action of hindering the Spirit should cease. There can be no achievement of the moral purpose of God in the life of the believer apart from an intimate and vital relationship between the guidance and direction of the Spirit and the life of the individual.

Yieldedness to the will of God implies first of all yieldedness to the Word of God and the standards of moral excellence which are set forth in the Scriptures. Many issues which face the Christian, however, are not taught explicitly in the Bible. Hence, second, there must be yieldedness to the guidance of the Holy Spirit. The Holy Spirit is given to the individual to provide guidance in these matters. That is, His purpose is to apply the general principles of the Bible to the particular issue which is facing the individual.

Third, in addition to being yielded to the Word of God and to the guidance of the Holy Spirit, yieldedness implies adjustment to the providential acts of God, whether it be of the nature of Paul's "thorn in the flesh," or anything else which might prompt rebellion against God's dealings with His child. The believer must be willing to accept divinely appointed situations, although he is still free to pray and ask God to change them. The role of the Spirit in comforting the believer is often related to providential situations in which, contrary to the believer's own desire, God is fulfilling His purpose in providing a means and context for life which ordinarily would not be the situation of human choosing.

The supreme illustration of such yieldedness, is, of course, Jesus Christ. This is described in Philippians 2:5-11, and speaks of His condescension and humility. Christ is revealed as being willing to be what God wanted Him to be, willing to do what God wanted Him to do, and willing to go where God wanted Him to go. In a similar measure, Christians in the will of God may have unpleasant tasks to perform which require yieldedness of heart and the sustaining grace of the Holy Spirit. Like Christ, the believer must say, "Not my will, but thine, be done" (Lk 22:42). Moral excellence in the life of the believer is inseparable from a vital communication and empowerment of the indwelling Holy Spirit which is only possible when the believer is yielded to the Holy Spirit.

VITAL FELLOWSHIP WITH THE SPIRIT

A second major factor in achieving holiness is fellowship with the Holy Spirit. The partnership of the believer and the indwelling Holy Spirit in all that is undertaken for God is absolutely essential to achieve the will of God. This in turn depends upon intimate fellowship between the Spirit and the believer. The entrance of rebellion and a continued state of being unyielded to the Holy Spirit will greatly harm and hinder the communication of the will of God and the power to accomplish it.

It is because of this obvious requirement for achieving excellence in moral experience that the believer is exhorted in Ephesians 4:30, "Grieve not the Holy Spirit of God, whereby ye are sealed unto the day of redemption." This command directs our attention first of all to the fact that the Holy Spirit is a person who has intellect, sensibility (feeling), and will. The Holy Spirit has feelings and is sensitive to the presence of sin in the life of a believer. Rebellion against the direction of the Holy Spirit in the life constitutes an offense to His holy character and can result in great loss to the individual believer.

Grieving the Holy Spirit originates in quenching the Spirit or hindering the Spirit's direction and empowering of the Christian life. Persistence in this results in loss of intimate fellowship and of the full ministry of the Spirit to the individual. He no longer is filled with the Spirit, empowered by the Spirit, or taught by the Spirit, and in various degrees he is removed from the effective ministry of the Spirit to him. The result is that the Christian is thrown on his natural resources and often may act like a person who is not a Christian.

The emotional life of the believer may have its ups and downs, quite apart from the matter of spiritual fellowship with the Holy Spirit, and physical weariness, discouraging experiences, and hunger or pain may affect the spiritual experience of the spiritual life. The long-range effects of walking without the Spirit's direction and power, however, soon become evident to both the Christian and those who observe his life. It is probably true that the great majority of Christians have in some measure grieved the Holy Spirit and are living on limited enablement in the spiritual life.

The decline of a person's spiritual experience because of

grieving the Holy Spirit does not affect his relationship to God in grace nor does it affect the certainty of his eternal salvation. Because a true believer is the object of divine grace, there is always the open door back into fellowship through confession of sin. According to 1 John 1:9, the remedy for having grieved the Holy Spirit is found in genuine confession of sin with the promise that, "If we confess our sins, he is faithful and just to forgive us our sins, and to cleanse us from all unrighteousness." This assurance and invitation is given in a book of the Bible dedicated to the revelation of fellowship with God and is directed immediately to Christians. Confession of sin on the part of an unsaved person would not in itself provide forgiveness or salvation. The text presumes that there is already a relationship to God in grace to which appeal can be made. The forgiveness is not a matter of law or legal obligation, but rather a relationship between a father and his child. Just as for unsaved people the exhortation is summed up in the word "believe," so for the Christian who has grieved the Holy Spirit his obligation is summed up in the word "confess."

It is obvious that confession must be genuine, it must be from the heart, and in the nature of the case it involves judging the sin as sin which has grieved the Holy Spirit. Confession by its very nature involves self-judgment as brought out in 1 Corinthians 11:31. The text according to 1 John 1:9, however, assures the believer that upon confession he can be sure of forgiveness because God is faithful to His promise and just, inasmuch as Christ has died for sin.

Confession is on the human side and reflects the adjustment that is necessary in human experience and personality to restore the marred fellowship with God. According to 1 John 2:1-2, it is clear that on the divine side the adjustment has been already made. Christ as the Advocate of the believer has already interceded for him for "he is the propitiation for our sins: and not for our's only, but also for the sins of the whole world" (1 Jn 2:2). Inasmuch as the divine side is always in proper adjustment, a Christian out of fellowship is obligated to perform his own act of confession. Thus he is able to be restored into close fellowship with the Lord.

The necessity of a close fellowship with the Holy Spirit through yieldedness of heart and confession of known sin is indispensable to achieving the moral excellence required for a life that is truly honoring to God. Christians are solemnly warned that those who trifle with their moral obligations may subject themselves to God's own discipline. As illustrated in the Corinthian church, Christians are warned, "If we would judge ourselves, we should not be judged. But when we are judged, we are chastened of the Lord, that we should not be condemned with the world" (1 Co 11:31-32). God permits His child time in which to evaluate his life, judge his sin, confess it, and be restored into fellowship. Failure to do so, however, invites the chastening judgment of God. As was true in the Corinthian church, it is possible for Christians to suffer physical illness and even death as a result of failure to walk in fellowship with God and to avail themselves of the open door of restoration. It is so unnecessary for Christians to suffer needlessly as brought out in 1 Peter 4:14-15 where Peter states, "Let none of you suffer as a murderer, or as a thief, or as an evildoer, or as a busybody in other men's matters."

THE MINISTRY OF THE SPIRIT

The solution of the moral problem in the Christian life is found in the Holy Spirit's filling the life of the believer and enabling him to achieve the miracle of a God-honoring life. It is clear, however, that the ministry of the Spirit to a yielded believer who is walking in fellowship with the Holy Spirit has tremendous effects upon the total life of the believer—all of which are related in one way or another to the moral issue. An important result of the ministry of the Spirit to the believer is that he is taught the things of God. Christ in the upper room prophesied that the Spirit would teach His own. He told His disciples, "When he, the Spirit of truth, is come, he will guide you into all truth: for he shall not speak of himself; but whatsoever he shall hear, that shall he speak: and he will shew you things to come. He shall glorify me: for he shall receive of mine, and shall shew it unto you" (Jn 16:13-14). The Spirit of God is the master teacher, who, as the omniscient God, can guide the Christian in the comprehension of all the truth. As such, He will not speak primarily of Himself, but shall be a means of communicating to the believer that which God wants him to know. It is most significant that His primary task is to glorify Christ or to magnify the perfections of Christ and make Him real and precious to the believer.

Another major passage dealing with the teaching ministry of the Spirit is found in 1 Corinthians 2:9—3:2. Here revelation is given that the believer in Christ is taught things by the Spirit which cannot be known by man naturally. This requires, on the part of the pupil, however, that he be teachable—that is, he must be sensitive and listening to the voice of the Holy Spirit. The Corinthians who were carnal or fleshly were able only to receive the milk of the Word—the partial and simple truths that were related to their limited spiritual experience. Inasmuch as comprehension of the truth of God is essential for intelligent life and service, so a walk of fellowship with the Spirit in which the divine Teacher can display the things of God is an important aspect of God's present program for His own.

The ministry of the Spirit is not only to instruct Christians in the revelation of the Word of God and in understanding of what might be called normative truth, but the ministry of the Spirit is also to apply this to the particular situation of the individual Christian in the form of guidance in decisions that need to be made. It is only as the Christian is a living sacrifice, transformed by the renewing of his mind and not conformed to this world, that he is able to "prove what is that good, and acceptable, and perfect, will of God" (Ro 12:2). Guidance is given those who are already committed to the will of God as illus-trated in the servant of Abraham who testified in his search for a bride for Isaac, "I being in the way, the LORD led me to the house of my master's brethren" (Gen 24:27). Guidance is not only the privilege but the mark of a true believer as brought out in Romans 8:14, "For as many as are led by the Spirit of God, they are the sons of God." The leading of the Spirit according to Galatians 5:18 is far superior to direction by the law in that it is personal and adapted to the individual life.

One of the by-products of the ministry of the Spirit to each believer is that he has assurance of salvation. According to Romans 8:16, "The Spirit itself beareth witness with our spirit, that we are the children of God." The same thought is brought out in Galatians 4:6, 1 John 3:24, and 1 John 4:13. Obviously a real intimate fellowship with the Holy Spirit speaks of a re-lationship which includes salvation and brings comfort and joy to the believer because of his present and future salvation.

In like measure the presence of the Holy Spirit leads the be-liever into a true worship of God and an admiration of the infinite perfections of our God. The believer who is filled with the Spirit is able to enjoy worship, fulfilling the description, "Speaking to yourselves in psalms and hymns and spiritual songs, singing and making melody in your heart to the Lord; Giving thanks always for all things unto God and the Father in the name of our Lord Jesus Christ" (Eph 5:19-20). As the Spirit reveals the glories of Christ and the perfections of God, the believer is inspired by the Spirit to worship in spirit and in truth. Such exercise of heart is far superior to the rituals of man which often lack reality of experience.

The ministry of the Spirit to the believer also is related to his prayer life inasmuch as he needs to be guided in his prayer life, burdened by the love of God for others, and constrained to become involved in the prayer needs of those about him. Ac-cording to Romans 8:26, the Spirit also intercedes for Chris-tians "with groanings which cannot be uttered." Inasmuch as the Spirit is ministering to the believer as well as interceding for him, He can guide and direct the effective prayer exercise of a believer, presenting his petitions and worship to the Lord.

The ministry of the Spirit to the believer in all of these things —teaching, guiding, assuring, inspiring worship, and guiding prayer—is vitally related to the spiritual life and holiness of the individual believer and affects the quality of his life as it reflects the holiness of God.

The ministry of the Spirit also is manifested in holy works or service for God, and it is clear that only as the Holy Spirit works within an individual can he really have the bountiful life of service for others which is the Christian calling. This was anticipated by Christ in John 7:38-39 where He spoke of rivers of living water as proceeding from within the believer. Such an abundant blessing is not possible to man naturally and can only be fulfilled as the believer fulfills the good works for which he was created in Christ (Eph 2:10). The holy life of service is, therefore, also a result of the ministry of the Spirit in the life of the yielded believer and is related to the ministry of the Spirit to promote holiness in the life.

In addition to all these important aspects of spiritual life, it is obvious that the Holy Spirit of God also works in the character of the believer himself and produces in him the evidence of His working in the fruit of the Spirit. According to Galatians 5:22-23, in contrast to the works of the flesh, "The fruit of the Spirit is love, joy, peace, longsuffering, gentleness, goodness, faith, meekness, temperance: against such there is no law."

The entire work of the Holy Spirit is, therefore, related to the moral experience of the believer. This, of course, begins with his salvation which makes it possible for him to be released from the slavery of sin and able to choose the way of righteousness. The indwelling Holy Spirit is provided by God to give the enablement and provide the ministries which are necessary to the believer as he lives in this sinful world.

The most important aspect of the Holy Spirit in relation to

the moral life of the believer is found first of all in the necessity to yield to the Holy Spirit and to let Him direct, guide, and empower according to His will. The inevitable areas of failure which come into the life of the believer through unyieldedness and sin are bound to require confession of sin and restoration according to God's invitation. The child of God must be in fellowship with God through the Holy Spirit in order to achieve the high quality of moral experience which is expected of believers whose proper standard of life is the holiness of God Himself.

Many factors are related to the holiness of God as seen in the believer, including the ministry of the Spirit in teaching the truth of God, in guiding, in decisions based upon the normative truth of the Word of God, in worship, in prayer, in service, and finally in the transformation of the believer himself. The fruit of the Spirit is manifested through him, and that which is so contrary to the flesh becomes the dominant experience and fruitage of his spiritual experience. It is only when all these factors combine that true morality is achieved, and the believer's life is indeed that which reflects the glory and perfection of God's own infinite holiness. Although the experience of this is necessarily somewhat qualified and relative in this world, the believer is assured that his longing for complete conformity to the will and character of God will be fulfilled in eternity, even though only partially realized in time. The tragedy is, however, that so many are content with living in the lowlands when they could be having the joy and peace of Christian experience and the fruitage in their own lives and in the lives of others that comes from dependence upon the Holy Spirit. Holy living is possible only by the Holy Spirit.

4

The Spirit at Work in Spiritual Gifts

ONE OF THE IMPORTANT MINISTRIES of the Holy Spirit to believers today is the bestowal of spiritual gifts upon Christians at the time of their conversion. While Christians may have natural abilities even before they are saved, spiritual gifts seem to be related to the special purpose of God in calling them and saving them; and, in the language of Ephesians 2:10, they are "created in Christ Jesus unto good works, which God hath before ordained that we should walk in them."

Spiritual gifts are divinely given capacities to perform useful functions for God, especially in the area of spiritual service. Just as the human body has members with different capacities, so individual Christians forming the church as the body of Christ have different capacities. These help them contribute to the welfare of the church as a whole, as well as to bear an effective witness to the world. Spiritual gifts are bestowed by the sovereign choice of God and need to be exercised in the power and under the direction of the Holy Spirit.

Every Christian has at least some spiritual gifts, as according to 1 Corinthians 12:7, "The manifestation of the Spirit is given to every man to profit." After enumerating a partial list of such gifts, the apostle concludes in 1 Corinthians 12:11, "But all these worketh that one and the selfsame Spirit, dividing to every man severally as he will." The analogy of the human body is then developed as illustrating the various functions of members of the body of Christ.

Spiritual gifts obviously differ in value, and the list of gifts in 1 Corinthians 12:28 is given in the order of importance. In 1 Corinthians 13, the importance of the use of spiritual gifts in love is emphasized. Some gifts which were bestowed in the early church seem no longer to be operative today, and this introduces the important consideration of the extent of contemporary spiritual gifts.

SPIRITUAL GIFTS USED TODAY

Practically all serious expositors of the Word of God agree that some spiritual gifts continue throughout the age. These constitute the more important and essential capacities within the church which enable it to function and fulfill its divinely purposed role.

The gift of teaching or expounding the Scriptures is one of the more important gifts and is mentioned in Romans 12:7, 1 Corinthians 12:28, and Ephesians 4:11. Obviously the teaching of divine revelation to others is a most important function of the members of the body of Christ. Although all believers have the capacity by the Spirit to receive divine revelation as is taught in the Word of God, all do not have the same gift in communicating this truth to others. The teaching gift does not necessarily require superior knowledge, but it does require the capacity for successful communication and application of the truth to the individual. No doubt the gift of teaching natural truth is similar to that of teaching spiritual truth, but the spiritual gift is especially adaptable to teaching the Word of God. Hence a person might be quite gifted in teaching natural truth who would not be effective in teaching the Word of God.

A common gift among Christians is that of ministering one to the other—mentioned in Romans 12:7 and 1 Corinthians 12:28. This gift varies a great deal depending on the person and the situation, and some are able to minister in one way and some in another. The total work of God depends upon the capacity of the members of the body of Christ to minister in this way.

The gift of administration is related to wise direction of the work of God in the church and is mentioned in Romans 12:7 and in 1 Corinthians 12:28. Comparatively few Christians are able administrators in the realm of spiritual things, and those lacking this gift should seek direction and guidance of those who have it.

The gift of evangelism mentioned in Ephesians 4:11 refers to unusual capacity to preach the gospel of salvation and to win the lost to Christ. While every Christian should be a channel of information to others and should do the work of an evangelist as Timothy was instructed to do (2 Ti 4:5), nevertheless, some will be more effective in preaching the gospel than others.

The gift of being a pastor or shepherd of the flock also calls for special abilities. In Ephesians 4:11, pastors and teachers are linked, indicating that a true shepherd will also be able to teach or feed his flock, and that a true teacher should have some pastoral abilities. While these qualities may be found in various degrees in different individuals, the link between teaching and shepherding the flock is inevitable for one who wants to be effective in preaching the Word of God.

The gift of exhortation mentioned in Romans 12:8 has the thought of presenting the truth in such a way as to stir to action. Sometimes those who have a gift of exhortation are not necessarily good Bible teachers, and vice versa; and men with varied gifts are all essential to the work of the church.

Some less important gifts are also mentioned in the Bible, such as the gift of giving, or having the special grace of sharing earthly possessions as mentioned in Romans 12:8. The gift of showing mercy relates to the special ability to show empathy and sympathy for those in need and is mentioned in Romans 12:8. The gift of faith, or that of special trust in the Lord, is included in 1 Corinthians 12:8-10. All of these gifts abide throughout the entire church age and constitute the divinely appointed enablement for the church to fulfill its task.

SPIRITUAL GIFTS WHICH ARE TEMPORARY

The question as to whether certain spiritual gifts are temporary is one of the debated areas of truth relating to the Holy Spirit in the contemporary church. While most of the church will agree that certain spiritual gifts were discontinued after the apostolic age, others are insisting that gifts given at the beginning of the church age continue in the same way throughout the entire period.

On the surface it is quite clear that the modern church does not function quite like the apostolic church. There is an evident decline in miracles, though God is still able to perform the miraculous. No longer does the testimony of the church depend upon its capacity to support its oral testimony by phenomenal miraculous works. It is also clear from the history of the Bible that miracles were evident for particular purposes in some periods while almost absent in others. Three notable periods of miracles are mentioned specifically in the Bible, that is, (1) the period of Moses, (2) the period of Elijah and Elisha, and (3) the period of Christ and the apostles. In each of these periods there was a need to authenticate the message that God gave his prophets, but once this need was met, the miracles seemed to recede.

The problems relating to the question of whether some gifts are temporary have been focused principally on the gift of tongues, the gift of interpreting tongues, and the gifts of miracles or healing. Relatively little controversy has been aroused concerning whether or not certain other spiritual gifts were only temporary.

It seems evident from the Scriptures that the gift of apostleship was limited to the first-century church. Apostles were distinguished from prophets and teachers in 1 Corinthians 12:28. During the apostolic period they had unusual authority and were the channels of divine revelation. Often they had the gift of prophecy as well as that of working miracles. Generally speaking, those who were in the inner circle of the apostles were eyewitnesses of the resurrection of Christ or, like Paul, had seen Christ subsequent to His resurrection. In Protestantism, comparatively few claims have been advanced that any exist today with the same apostolic gift as was found in the early church.

The gift of prophecy, although claimed by a few, generally speaking, has also been recognized as having only passing validity. In the early church prior to the completion of the New Testament, authoritative revelation was needed from God not only concerning the present where the prophet was a forthteller but also concerning the future where the prophet was a foreteller. The Scriptures themselves contain illustrations of such prophetic offices and their exercise. The gift is mentioned in Romans 12:6, 1 Corinthians 12:10, and 1 Corinthians 14:1-40. A number of illustrations are found as in the case of Agabus who predicted a famine (Ac 11:27-28), and who warned Paul of coming sufferings (Ac 21:10-11). Among the prophets and teachers at Antioch according to Acts 13:1 were Barnabas, Simeon, Lucius, Manaen, and Paul. Women could also be prophets, as illustrated in the four daughters of Philip (Ac 21:9). Paul clearly had the prophetic gift, as manifested in Acts 16:6-10, 18:9-10, 22:17-21 and 27:23-24. Among the others who were evidently prophets were Judas and Silas (Ac 15:32). All of these were used as authoritative channels through which God could give divine revelations sometimes about the contemporary situation and sometimes about the future.

New Testament prophets were like prophets in the Old Testament who spoke for God, warned of judgment, and delivered the message from God, whether contemporary or predictive. The Old Testament prophet, however, was more of a national leader, reformer, and patriot, and his message usually was to Israel alone. In the New Testament the prophet principally ministered to the church and did not have national characteristics.

In order to be a prophet the individual had to have a message from God in the form of special revelation, had to have guidance regarding its declaration so that it would be given forth accurately, and the message itself had to have the authority of God. The prophetic office, therefore, was different from the teaching office in that the teaching office had no more authority than the Scripture upon which it was based, whereas the prophetic office had its authority in the experience of divine reception and communication of truth.

In the early church the prophetic office was very important and was considered one of the principal gifts. It is discussed somewhat at length in 1 Corinthians 14, and given more prominence than other gifts in the list in 1 Corinthians 12:8-10. Because no one today has the same authority or the experience of receiving normative truth, it is highly questionable whether anyone has the gift of prophecy today. No one has come forward to add even one verse of normative truth to the Bible. While individuals can have specific guidance and be given insight to the meaning of Scripture, no one is given truth that is not already contained in the Bible itself. Accordingly, it may be concluded that the gift of prophecy has ceased.

The gift of miracles, while a prominent gift in the early church (1 Co 12:28) and frequently found in the New Testament, does not seem to exist today in the same way that it did in Bible times. Throughout the earthly ministry of Christ, hundreds of miracles were performed in attestation of His divine power and Messianic office. After the ascension of Christ into heaven, miraculous works continued in the early church, on many occasions attending the preaching of the Word and constituting proof that it was indeed from God. With the completion of the New Testament, the need for such miraculous evidence in support of the preached Word seems to have

ceased and the authority and convicting power of the Spirit
seems to have replaced these outer manifestations.

In holding that the gift of miracles is temporary, it is not
taught that there are no miracles today, as God still is able to
do supernaturally anything He wills to do. It is rather that in
the purpose of God miracles no longer constitute a mainline
evidence for the truth, and individuals do not (as in the apostolic times) have the gift of miracles. While some who claim
to have the gift of miracles today have succeeded in convincing
many of their supernatural powers, the actual investigation of
their operation, which in some cases may be supported by individual miracles here and there, is often found to be quite
deceptive, and often the alleged healings are psychologically
instead of supernaturally effected. The thought is not that God
cannot perform miracles today, but rather that it is not His purpose to give to individuals the power to perform miracles by
the hundreds as was true in apostolic periods.

What is true of the gift of miracles in general seems also to
be true of the gift of healing mentioned in 1 Corinthians 12:9,
28 and 30. In biblical times there were special acts of divine
healing, and undoubtedly there were hundreds of instances
where the apostles were able to demonstrate the divine power
that was within them by restoring health to those who had various physical disabilities.

A survey of the present church, while not without its seg-
ment of those who claim divine healing, does not support the
contention that it is the same gift as was given in the early
church. That God has the power to heal supernaturally today
is obvious, and that there may be cases of supernatural healing
is not to be denied. Healing as a divine method for communication or authenticating the truth, however, is not the present
divine purpose, and those who claim to have the gift of healing
have again and again been proved to be spurious in their claims.
While Christians should feel free to pray and to seek divine
healing from God, it is also true that frequently it is God's will

even for the most godly of people, that, like Paul, they should continue in their afflictions as the means to the end of demonstrating the sufficiency of God. Cases of healing are relatively rare in the modern church and are not intended to be a means of evangelism.

Probably the most controversial of the gifts of the Spirit in the contemporary doctrine of the Holy Spirit is the gift of tongues. According to Acts 2:1-13, on the day of Pentecost, Jews who had come to Jerusalem for the feast were amazed to hear the apostles speak in their language, and they asked the question, "How hear we every man in our own tongue, wherein we were born? Parthians, and Medes, and Elamites, and the dwellers in Mesopotamia, and in Judaea, and Cappadocia, in Pontus, and Asia, Phrygia, and Pamphylia, in Egypt, and in the parts of Libya about Cyrene, and strangers of Rome, Jews and proselytes, Cretes and Arabians, we do hear them speak in our tongues the wonderful works of God" (Ac 2:8-11). This was clearly a supernatural work of God and a testimony to the authority and truth of the apostles' message concerning Jesus Christ.

Two other instances occurred in Acts—one in Acts 10:46 on the occasion of Peter speaking to the house of Cornelius and the other in Acts 19. In Acts 11 Peter, analyzing their speaking in tongues, said, "And as I began to speak, the Holy Ghost fell on them, as on us at the beginning" (Ac 11:15). In the instance mentioned in Acts 19 when Paul encountered certain disciples of John the Baptist at Ephesus, as Paul "laid his hands upon them, the Holy Ghost came on them; and they spake with tongues, and prophesied" (Ac 19:6). It would seem reasonable to conclude that in all of these three instances in Acts there was a supernatural manifestation of the Spirit in the form of empowering men to speak in languages which were not known to them. It should also be observed, however, that these are the only three instances mentioned in the book of Acts, and that apart from the discussion in 1 Corinthians 12-

14 there is no other reference to speaking in tongues in the New Testament. What is the explanation of this gift, and can it be exercised today?

Although some writers have distinguished between the instances in Acts which were clearly in known languages and the experience of the Corinthians in 1 Corinthians 12-14, there does not seem to be adequate basis for this distinction, as the same expressions are used in both places. The term "unknown tongue" as in the King James Version in 1 Corinthians 14:2 is inaccurate, since the word "unknown" is not in the original. There is no evidence that the gift of tongues used languages that were unknown to men, although there is reference to the theoretical possibility of speaking in the tongues of angels in 1 Corinthians 13:1. The instance in Acts 2 was clearly in known languages as the recognition of a language as a known language is essential to any scientific confirmation that genuine speaking in tongues has taken place. If those speaking in tongues had only babbled incoherent sounds, this would lend itself to fraudulent interpretation which could not in any way be checked. Accordingly, it should be assumed that speaking in tongues in the Bible was a genuine gift, that it involved speaking in existing languages unknown to the speaker, and that actual communication took place in such experiences. Hence, genuine speaking in tongues cannot be explained simply by hypnosis or psychological emotionalism, but has to be recognized as a genuine gift of the Holy Spirit.

The purpose of speaking in tongues is clearly defined in the Scriptures. It was intended to be a sign in attestation to the gospel and a proof of the genuineness of the work of the Holy Spirit (1 Co 14:22). Although words were expressed and the glory of God was revealed, there is no instance in Scripture where a doctrine was revealed through speaking in tongues, and it does not seem to have been a major vehicle for revelation of new truth.

In all three instances in Acts, speaking in tongues served to prove that what was taking place was a genuine work of God. In Acts 2, of course, it was the gift of the Spirit and the beginning of the New Testament church. In Acts 10 it was necessary as an evidence to Peter of the genuineness of the work of salvation in the household of Cornelius and was designed to teach Peter that the gospel was universal in its invitation. The third instance, in Acts 19, again served to identify the twelve men mentioned as actually being converted to Christianity instead of simply being followers of John the Baptist. In all of the instances in Acts, speaking in tongues was a sign that the work of the Holy Spirit was genuine.

The only passage in the New Testament that deals theologically with the gift of tongues is found in 1 Corinthians 12-14. In the Corinthian church, plagued with so many doctrinal and spiritual problems, it is rather significant that three chapters of Paul's epistle to them are devoted to expounding the purpose and meaning of tongues, giving more attention to this problem than to any other which existed in the Corinthian church. On the whole, the chapters are designed to correct and regulate speaking in tongues rather than to exhort them to the exercise of this gift. In the light of the fact that none of the other epistles or New Testament books apart from the book of Acts deals at all with this subject, it would seem apparent that speaking in tongues, although it existed in the early church, was not a major factor in its evangelism, in its spiritual life, or in its demonstration of the power of God. It seems to have been prominent only in a church which was notoriously unspiritual (see 1 Co 1-11).

The gift of tongues is introduced in 1 Corinthians 12 as one of many gifts, and, significantly, as the least of the gifts enumerated in 1 Corinthians 12:28. It is number eight in the list, and immediately afterward the apostle makes it plain that spiritual gifts are not possessed by all the church, and only a few would necessarily speak in tongues. The entire next chapter of 1 Corinthians is devoted to motivation in speaking in tongues, and Paul points out that the only proper motivation is love. Accordingly, they were not to exalt the gift and they were not to use it as a basis for spiritual pride. Speaking in tongues without love was an empty and ineffectual exercise.

In chapter 14 the discussion on the significance of the gift of tongues deals with the subject in some detail. At least five major points are made. First, tongues is defined as a gift which is not nearly as important as other gifts such as the gift of teaching or the gift of prophecy. The problem was that speaking in tongues could not be understood by anybody without the gift of interpretation and was limited in its capacity to communicate divine revelation. Paul accordingly says that it is better to speak five words with understanding than ten thousand words in an unknown tongue (1 Co 14:19). It is clear from this that Paul exalts the gifts that actually communicate truth rather than the phenomenal gift of tongues which was more of a sign.

Second, it is pointed out that speaking in tongues should not be exercised in the assembly unless an interpreter is present. The principal exercise of speaking in tongues was to be in private, but even here Paul indicates that praying with understanding is better than praying in an unknown tongue (1 Co 14:15).

Third, the importance of speaking in tongues is found in the fact that it is a sign to unbelievers—that is, it is a demonstration of the supernatural power of God—and tongues is not primarily intended for the edification of believers (1 Co 14:21-22). The Corinthian church, however, was told that unless speaking in tongues was conducted with proper order, it would not achieve its purpose of convincing unbelievers but rather would introduce an element of confusion (1 Co 14:23). In the public assembly the exercise of the gift of prophecy, the communication of a revelation from God in a known language, was more important and more effectual in leading to faith and worship than the exercise of the gift of tongues (1 Co 14:24-25).

Fourth, spiritual gifts of speaking in tongues as well as the exercise of the gift of prophecy should be regulated and should not be allowed to dominate the assembly. The principle should be followed that these gifts should be exercised when it is for the edification of the church. Ordinarily only two or three in any given meeting should be allowed to speak in tongues, and none at all should be permitted if an interpreter is not present (1 Co 14:27-28). A blanket prohibition was laid down against women speaking either as a prophet or in tongues in the church assembly (1 Co 14:34-35). The general rule is applied that all things should be done decently and in order.

Fifth, Paul allows that speaking in tongues should be exercised and not forbidden, but its limitations should be recognized and its exercise should be in keeping with its value. From this thorough discussion of the gift of tongues in 1 Corinthians 14, as well as from the introductory two chapters, it is evident that speaking in tongues was not intended to be a primary source of revelation or a primary experience of power in the church. It was rather collateral and auxiliary as a proof of the truth of God.

If the speaking in tongues was truly exercised, however, in the early church and under proper regulation was beneficial, the question of course still remains as to whether a similar experience can be had by the church today. Because it is almost impossible to prove a universal negative in an experiential matter such as this, especially in the light of many who claim to have exercised the gift, a practical line of approach is first of all to examine the question as to whether the Scriptures themselves indicate that speaking in tongues was a temporary gift and then, on the basis of the total evidence, to ask the question as to what one should do in the light of the claims of many that they have a gift of speaking in tongues today.

There are at least four arguments leading to the conclusion that speaking in tongues is temporary. First, it is clear that there was no exercise of speaking in tongues before Pentecost.

Christ and the apostles and John the Baptist did not exercise the gift of speaking in tongues prior to Pentecost. There is no evidence that such a spiritual gift was given in the Old Testament period. Accordingly, it follows that if such a gift was given at Pentecost it also could be withdrawn according to the sovereign will of God.

Second, according to the Scriptures, tongues was especially to be a sign to Israel. Isaiah 28:11 prophesied, "For with stammering lips and another tongue will he speak to this people." This is quoted in 1 Corinthians 14:21-22 as being fulfilled in the exercise of the speaking in tongues. Such a sign gift would be fitting and effective at the beginning of a new age, but it would not necessarily be required throughout a long period of time.

Third, although it is debated, it seems evident that some other spiritual gifts, such as the gift of apostleship, the gift of prophecy, the gift of miracles, and the gift of healing, were temporary. If these gifts, so effective in establishing the church, were used in the apostolic period but seem to fade thereafter, it would follow that the gift of tongues might have a similar withdrawal from the church.

Fourth, the statement is made in 1 Corinthians 13:8 that tongues would cease. It can be debated, of course, as to whether this means that the gift of tongues will cease now or whether it will cease at some future time. The point, however, is that in either case, speaking in tongues is temporary and not a manifestation continued indefinitely in the purpose of God. These evidences seem to point to the conclusion that speaking in tongues is not a gift which can be expected to be exercised throughout the entire church period.

The natural question is, How can we account for the exercise of speaking in tongues today as it is claimed by many individuals? Some sort of a phenomenon which is identified as speaking in tongues is a manifest feature of contemporary Christianity. Three explanations are possible.

First, much of the phenomenon of speaking in tongues today seems by all normal tests to be babbling without known words or language. Such can be completely explained by psychological means and without supernatural inducement.

Second, claims are made in some cases that speaking in tongues is in definite languages recognizable by those who are familiar with these languages. Although such claims are few and far between and hard to demonstrate, if such a claim can be substantiated the question is, How can it be explained? This introduces a second possibility for explaining a portion at least of the tongues phenomena today.

It seems clear that Satan is able to counterfeit the gift of tongues, and occasional reports are received of those claiming to speak in tongues who actually express the most horrible blasphemies against God.

A third possibility in explaining the contemporary claim for speaking in tongues is, of course, to recognize that, in some rather remote instances, it is a genuine spiritual gift. Many evangelical Christians do not feel that there has ever been evidence in our century of the exercise of the genuine gift; but if such could be substantiated in a particular case, it still would not justify the great majority of instances of speaking in tongues —which apparently are not at all what the Scriptures refer to as speaking in tongues.

Much of the difficulty in the modern Pentecostal movement is found in the fact that rarely will it submit the exercise of the speaking in tongues to scientific demonstration. If a given instance of speaking in tongues were put on electronic tape and played separately to several individuals who claim to have the gift of interpretation, and their translations proved to be identical, it would be a scientific demonstration of the genuineness of speaking in tongues such as was true on the day of Pentecost. Unfortunately the Pentecostal movement has not, as far as the author knows, been willing to submit speaking in tongues to such a scientific test. Until they do, they continue to cause

questions to be raised as to the genuineness of the exercise of
the gift of tongues in the contemporary situation.

It is also obvious that while speaking in tongues was a genuine gift in the early church, it was peculiarly adapted to abuse.
In the Corinthian church it was a source of pride on the part
of unspiritual people who exercised the gift but who had little
spiritual power or holiness attending its exercise. Unfortunately, the same tendencies sometimes are observed today in those
who claim to speak in tongues but who make it a source of
pride instead of effective testimony for the Lord. It is not true,
as often claimed, that speaking in tongues is a proof of either
the filling of the Spirit or of spiritual power. There is no basis
for pride in the exercise of such a gift.

The danger of the abuse of tongues may be itemized as existing in four areas. First, speaking in tongues is not, as is sometimes claimed today, a prominent spiritual gift. It is the least
of all spiritual gifts and is the least effective in propagating
Christianity.

Second, tongues is not a required sign of salvation and, by
its very nature as a gift, would be given only to a few, not to
all Christians. The lack of reference outside the books of Acts
and 1 Corinthians is substantial proof that it was not an important feature of experiential Christianity in the first century.

Third, it is quite clear that speaking in tongues is not in itself a proof of spirituality. The church that seems to have
exercised it the most was the least spiritual. The history of the
tongues movement seems to have given rise to emotionalism
and excesses of various sorts which have not been beneficial to
the propagation of the gospel.

Fourth, it is not true that speaking in tongues is an inseparable evidence of the baptism of the Spirit. Since it was a genuine
gift in the early church, one who spoke in tongues obviously
was also baptized into the body of Christ. Yet it is quite clear
from 1 Corinthians 12:13 that every Christian is baptized by
the Spirit into the body of Christ, but only a few speak in

tongues. Accordingly, the attempt to make tongues a necessary sign of either spirituality or salvation is an abuse of the doctrine which is expressly prohibited in the Scriptures.

A practical approach to the problem of speaking in tongues is probably not one of attempting to prove to Pentecostals that they do not have the gift, although this may be our own conclusion. It is rather than evangelical Christianity should insist that Pentecostalism should confine the exercise of their supposed gift of tongues to the regulations and limitations imposed by the Scriptures themselves. Obviously, if the Pentecostal movement followed closely the regulations laid down in 1 Corinthians 12-14, there would be little harm, if any, in exercising the supposed gift, for it would be regulated and kept within bounds and properly evaluated. The improper use and promotion of the gift of tongues, however, is detrimental to the exposition of Bible doctrine as a whole and confuses the issues of both salvation and spirituality.

If the gift of tongues is suspect as far as contemporary exercise is concerned, it also follows that the gift of interpreting tongues today is suspect. Because of the nature of the gift of interpreting tongues, it is difficult to check on it, but if a bona fide case could be found of one who without knowledge of a foreign language would be able to interpret such a foreign language while exercising the gift of tongues, and this in turn could be checked by someone who knows the language naturally, there would be scientific evidence for a supernatural gift. There still would be a possible question as to whether this was of God or of Satan. Until proof has been established as to the nature of the interpretation, it is reasonable to question whether the gift can be exercised today.

The gift of discerning spirits, while not related to speaking in tongues, is another gift that seems to have been temporary in the church. This was the gift of discerning whether a person supposedly speaking by the Spirit was speaking of God or of Satan. It is probably true that Christians today who are spiritually minded can discern whether one is Spirit directed or demon possessed, but this ability does not seem to be bestowed upon the church today as a particular gift.

In approaching these controversial matters, Christians should avail themselves of the revelation of Scripture and attempt to find a workable basis for solving these problems. The important truth is that there are spiritual gifts bestowed on the church today. The proper use of these gifts in the power of the Spirit is essential to fulfilling the work of God in and through His church. While the temporary gifts are no longer necessary to the testimony of God, the exercise of the permanent gifts is vitally important and the best demonstration of the power of the Holy Spirit.

5

The Spirit at Work in the Spirit-filled Life

ONE OF THE GREATEST NEEDS in the church today is the power of the Holy Spirit. Man in his natural ability is not able to serve God acceptably. Even if he has been renewed through salvation by the Spirit, this in itself does not assure him spiritual power in his life. Apart from the work of the Holy Spirit, a believer is not able to use effectively the gift of teaching and is not able to interpret God's guidance to him or in other ways to make effective the grace of God. It is for this reason the believer is commanded to "walk in the Spirit" (Gal 5:16).

LEARNING TO WALK BY THE SPIRIT

In exhorting the believer to walk by the Spirit, the concept is advanced that the Christian life can be accomplished only by the power of the Holy Spirit. Walking implies progress and direction. Each step is an incipient fall, as the body is supported by one limb and then the other. The verb "walk" in Galatians 5:16 is in the present tense and has the thought of "keep on walking," or continuously walking, by the Holy Spirit. The Greek for "by the Spirit" is the dative, *pneumati*, best translated as "by the Spirit" instead of "in the Spirit," as in the King James Version. While it is true that the believer is walking in the sphere of the Spirit, the thought is rather that it is by the Spirit's enablement that the believer is able to accomplish the high standard of the Christian walk. As the life of a Christian unfolds step by step, each foot of progress must be marked by the sustaining power and ministry of the Holy Spirit. Learning to walk by the Spirit is realized when one walks in dependence on and is supported by the presence and power of the Holy Spirit.

WHY WALK BY THE SPIRIT?

In the light of New Testament standards for the Christian life, which are far beyond anything the natural man could attain, it is obvious that only by the grace of God and the indwelling presence of the Holy Spirit can a measure of attainment be achieved in keeping with the will of God for the believer. Accordingly, the believer is exhorted to be holy as God is holy (1 Pe 1:16), and to love as Christ loved (Jn 13:34). As both experience and Scripture demonstrate, man beset by constant temptation and opposition to the holy life could never even partially attain this high standard of conduct apart from the grace and power of the Holy Spirit.

The obstacles confronted by the Christian in the Christian walk are massive and frontal. A Christian is living in a world system which is utterly contrary to the things of God. He is under constant influence to love the world, to compromise with the world, and to conform to the world. In himself, the Christian does not have the resources to confront such a formidable foe and needs the power and presence of the Holy Spirit.

In addition to the world itself, the Christian also encounters Satan as his arch enemy. The warfare with Satan is very real for anyone who attempts to lead a Christian life, and Paul bears witness to wrestling not with flesh and blood but with satanic powers in Ephesians 6:11-18. Satan not only blinds the minds of unbelievers (2 Co 4:4) but, like a roaring lion, is seeking whom he may devour (1 Pe 5:8). He is deceptive, often appearing as an angel of light (2 Co 11:14), and according to Christ is both a liar and a murderer (Jn 8:44). Against such an enemy whose wisdom and power far exceed the resources of an individual Christian, there could be no victory apart from the power and grace of God.

In addition to the confrontation of both the world and Satan, a Christian is faced with his own inner weakness. Although a Christian has a new nature and a new life in Christ, the old nature is still there trying to reassert itself and gain control. As Paul makes clear in Romans 6 and 7, in his own resources he was helpless to contend against such an inner betrayer and needed the power of the Spirit to gain victory. It is a marvelous testimony to the grace of God that believers with all these problems can nevertheless have a life that is glorifying to God if they are empowered by the Spirit.

PITFALLS TO HOLY LIVING

In seeking to realize the holy life in Christ and to translate the power of the Holy Spirit into living experience, it is all too easy to go to excesses in one direction or another. One of the pitfalls to the holy life is the concept that it is possible to attain sinless perfection in this life.

At the outset it is clear that the standard for the Christian life is the perfect holiness of God. There can be no compromise on the ideal and no lowering of the standard. However, taking into consideration what man is in his total context, it is obviously impossible for man to fulfill continuously such a high standard. Hence perfectionism, defined as the doctrine that a state of complete freedom from sin is obtainable in earthly life, is an ideal which is never attained by man except in a relative sense. It is possible for man to avoid willful sin, at least for a time, or to be free from known sin; but the sin nature itself cannot be eradicated, and it is inevitable that attainment of the standard will be marred by imperfection.

A study of the words containing the concept of "perfect" in both the Old and New Testaments makes plain that perfection is not considered to be sinless perfection. In general the thought of perfection in the Bible is that of being complete or properly adjusted. A second thought often presented is that of perfection in the sense of reaching a goal and hence has the concept of attainment. As both completeness and attainment are relative terms, so also is the concept of perfection.

The concept of perfection in the Bible is further considered under three aspects. Sometimes perfection is considered as positional, as in Hebrews 10:14 where it is stated, "For by one offering he hath perfected for ever them that are sanctified." This indicates that we have a perfect position in Christ.

A second aspect of perfection relates to spiritual maturity which is relative. In Philippians 3:15 the Philippians were exhorted, "Let us, therefore, as many as be perfect, be thus minded." He is referring to spiritual maturity and not sinless perfection, because in verse 12 in the same passage he plainly states that he has not reached ultimate perfection. Spiritual maturity, like physical maturity, indicates the person has reached full spiritual vigor, but not necessarily in infinite proportions. In Scripture, maturity is viewed in respect to various aspects of the will of God, such as knowing the will of God (Col. 4:12), love (1 Jn 4:17-18), personal holiness (2 Co 7:1), patience (Ja 1:4), and various good works (Heb 13:21). Spiritual maturity can also be viewed as progressive as in 2 Corinthians 7:1, where perfection is viewed as a process with the gifts bestowed upon the laborers being used for the perfecting of the saints (Eph 4:12). The concept of ultimate perfection is found in passages like Philippians 3:11-12, contemplating the results of resurrection from the dead and presentation in heaven. While the concept of ultimate perfection is therefore recognized, it is also plainly indicated that it is not obtainable prior to achieving the resurrection body.

The recognition that absolute perfection is impossible in this life should not deter the believer from doing all he can to measure up to the highest divine standard. It is for this purpose that the enablement of the Holy Spirit is provided, that the believer may be empowered to serve God and attain personal holiness.

Another approach to the concept of the holy life is afforded in the word "sanctification" itself. There are three main ideas presented in the Bible on sanctification—consecration or being set apart for holy use; separation, that is, distinction from that which is unholy; and purification, or the result of the cleansing process. Like the doctrine of perfection, sanctification is found in three tenses relating to (*a*) that which is positional; (*b*) that which is already perfect (the experiential or progressive type of sanctification in which a believer grows in holiness); and (*c*) the ultimate sanctification when he stands complete in the presence of God.

Positional holiness has by far the most references in the New Testament and is the thought in the use of the word "saint" which appears some sixty-five times. The emphasis in sanctification is that we already have a perfect standing or position (see Heb 10:14), and it is on this basis that we are called to bring our experience up to the standard as far as possible.

A few Scriptures refer to progressive sanctification as in John 17:17 where Christ prayed, "Sanctify them through thy truth: thy word is truth." The same thought is found in Ephesians 5:26 where the present ministry of Christ is revealed to be that of sanctifying His church by cleansing it by the washing of water by the Word of God (see also 1 Th 5:23). The concept of ultimate sanctification as a state is not expressly brought out in Scripture, but it is clear that when we are in heaven we will be completely set apart for holy use and will be like Christ (1 Jn 3:2). Similar passages are found in Ephesians 5:27 and Romans 8:29.

It may be concluded that while sanctification is, therefore, perfect in position, its experiential attainment is relative; and complete sanctification will be realized when we are in heaven where we will be completely set apart for holy use and will be like Christ (1 Jn 3:2).

It is most important to note from Scripture that for a believer to declare himself sinless, either in nature or in life, is to contradict both Scripture and experience, as 1 John 1:8 makes plain, "If we say that we have no sin, we deceive ourselves, and

the truth is not in us." The exhortations of the New Testament
teach that the path to victory over sin is not to arrive at a pla-
teau where sin is impossible, but rather through moment-by-
moment dependence on the power of the Holy Spirit to provide
deliverance. Those who claim sinless perfection are self-de-
ceived and, because of their supposed complete victory over
sin, tend to neglect the means of power provided by the Holy
Spirit. As 1 John 1:8 indicates, while they may deceive themselves, they do not deceive anyone else, as sinless perfection is
a crown which is unattainable in this life. To understand the
doctrine of sanctification properly is to open the door for the
power of the Holy Spirit to provide for the believer moment-
by-moment victory over sin.

Probably the most extreme of all the holiness doctrines is the
thought that the sin nature can be eradicated. In this concept
a Christian is not only declared not to sin, but it is claimed that
it is impossible for him to sin. Nothing should be more clear
in the New Testament than the fact that the spiritual life is one
of ceaseless warfare. Nowhere is the believer exhorted to attempt by any means whatever to eradicate the sin nature. Instead, the exhortations of Scripture constantly take into consideration that this is impossible and that victory over sin requires yieldedness to God and walking by the Spirit.

One of the contemporary erroneous concepts of holiness is
the theory that it is possible for a Christian to die completely
to self. Exhortations are sometimes made to the Christian to
crucify himself. The figure is not only unscriptural, but physi-
cally impossible since crucifixion must always be administered
by another. The error has arisen through an incorrect understanding of the tense of the verb in passages such as Romans
6:6. The verb is not in the present tense but correctly translated the passage reads, "Knowing this, that our old man was
crucified with him." The same is true with Galatians 2:20
where the perfect tense is used, signifying that not only are we
crucified with Christ already, but we have been crucified with

Him ever since Christ died upon the cross. The exhortation is to the point of recognizing this fact. It is impossible for a Christian by act of his will to die to self, but he can by the grace of God reckon himself dead to the sin nature which is still very much alive. By this he is disclaiming the right of the sin nature to rule over him in view of the power of God released through the death of Christ upon the cross. Christians who have foolishly concluded that they have actually died to self are soon disillusioned, as they find that the old nature is still very much alive and, apart from the power and grace of God, would again assert itself. The Christian life as a whole is so constituted that not only our salvation is completely dependent upon God and His grace, but also our daily victory is possible only as the reservoirs of divine power are released in the life of the Christian. This is what is meant by walking by the Spirit, letting the Spirit empower and direct and control.

WALKING BY THE POWER OF THE SPIRIT

In contrast to other exhortations to "quench not the Spirit" and to "grieve not the Spirit," walking by the power of the Holy Spirit is a positive command and is one of appropriation of what God has provided. It is the walk of the Spirit that produces contagious Christian experience, holiness of life, and a glorifying of God. It is only thus that holiness can be achieved and the fruit of the Spirit realized.

Walking by the Spirit is only possible as the Christian is first of all yielded to the Spirit of God, and, second, is walking in unhindered fellowship with the Spirit through confession of sin. Walking by the Spirit, however, is a positive moment-by-moment dependence upon the Spirit of God and what the Spirit of God can empower the Christian to do. The walk by the Spirit includes dependence upon the Word of God as providing the necessary standards of life and instruction in holy living. As one walks by the Spirit, he must be guided by the Spirit of God. Many moral issues are not dealt with explicitly in the

Scriptures, and the personal direction of an individual life into a proper sphere of service is possible only as the Spirit guides. Walking by the Spirit also implies dependence upon prayer, and spiritual power often is directly related to the prayer life of the believer. Walking by the Spirit is aided by fellowship with other believers who also are seeking the work of the Spirit in their lives. While the Spirit of God directly empowers, He also uses means in effecting in the individual life a perfect will of God.

Summary

IN THE GREAT PROGRAM of God for the redemption of the lost human race, the Scriptures make clear that Christ's death on the cross is God's provision for fallen humanity. Apart from this sacrifice there could be no permanent forgiveness, no release of the grace of God, and no relief from condemnation from sin. In the purpose of God it is also clear that salvation thus purchased by Christ is made effective by the Holy Spirit. It is only by the power of the Spirit that a lost soul can see and understand the gospel and believe. It is the power of the Holy Spirit revealed in salvation which delivers a person from his lost estate and makes him a new creature in Christ, possessing eternal life, indwelt by the Holy Spirit, and made one with the saints. Just as deliverance from sin and condemnation and our new position in Christ are made possible by the Holy Spirit, so the daily walk of the believer who experiences deliverance from sin and achieves a quality of life which brings glory to God is possible only as the Holy Spirit fills and empowers. God has made rich provision both for the salvation and the sanctification of those who come to Him through Christ. Those who have put their trust in Christ have the privilege and responsibility of availing themselves of this wonderful provision for joy and victory in Christ now, anticipating that perfect experience which will be theirs in heaven.